Charlie's Christmas Letter

Charlie's Christmas Letter

Things My Grandson Ought to Know

A. KINGSLEY WEATHERHEAD

RESOURCE *Publications* · Eugene, Oregon

CHARLIE'S CHRISTMAS LETTER
Things My Grandson Ought to Know

Resource Publications
An Imprint of Wipf and Stock Publishers
199 W. 8th Ave., Suite 3
Eugene, OR 97401
www.wipfandstock.com

ISBN 13: 978-1-60899-699-5

Manufactured in the U.S.A.

For Gerald and Gloria Johnson

Contents

Foreword

Dear Charlie,

Now that you are a teenager and now that Christmas is approaching I think it is time to give you answers to some of the questions which you, being a curious little kid, used to ask. For example, Why did Dad stick that bit of holly over the Van Gogh in the living room? you wanted to know. "Because it's Christmas," you were told—a dusty answer in place of a long story. Why did Santa have to come down the chimney instead of through the door or at least through a window? "Good question, Charlie." But good question unanswered; it's another long story. Or, when seeing a card from your aunt, the question, "Why do they have camels in Seattle?" deserved a better answer than, "Oh, Charlie, do be quiet!" from your mother, busy at the door, giving his Christmas tip to the boy who brings back the dry cleaning. I wonder if you can remember, Charlie, now you are older, all the mysteries that a perceptive child must face. And everyone's too busy at Christmas.

Then beside those details, closely or distantly related to the birth of Jesus, there are other things going on in the Christmas season, like the *Messiah,* which you were dragged out to hear one snowy night when you wanted to watch TV; and the *Nutcracker* ballet; and Charles Dickens' *Christmas Carol.* You ought to know something too about

what your Jewish friends are celebrating while you are doing Christmas. These things and more I want to tell you
about. So settle down on the couch, Charlie, leaning on one
elbow as you love to do, and start reading.

1

The Nativity

INTRODUCTION TO THE BIBLE NEWS

WHEN WE talk about Christmas, there are two things you have to remember from the beginning: first, the story of the nativity of Christ comes in two of the gospels in the New Testament, Matthew's and Luke's. "Gospel" means good news, and the news is a bit like the news we get today from whatever source: not altogether reliable. Remember, neither of the two people who wrote those two gospels and described the birth and what was going on around it had actually been there at the time; they didn't know Jesus' parents, and they hadn't witnessed first hand what really happened on that amazing occasion. They were not there; they were probably not yet born. The events they describe had taken place some fifty or more years before they wrote their stories. It's as if we were just now getting news of events from World War II or shortly thereafter from people who, though they knew about the war and had heard some of the details, hadn't been there themselves. There is no document in existence written by a contemporary of Jesus.

Then there is another complication: sometimes for the things we take to be part of Christmas there is no evidence in the gospels. Take for one instance the cow which is a feature of the crèche, the tableau of the nativity scene in the stable, said to have been pioneered by St. Francis of Assisi in the thirteenth century. Neither Luke nor Matthew mentions a cow in the stable where the child lay; its presence came from a prediction in the Old Testament, and thus it is in our crèches with the lineaments of adoration painted on its silken face. Its breath then and forever after became sweet, according to legend. And its presence in the stable has given rise also to the legend that on Christmas Eve the cattle in the fields fall on their knees. But it isn't in the gospel stories.

But then, more importantly, there are things in the gospels that are not at all what had actually happened, but what had been predicted to happen by prophets in the Old Testament. Thus throughout the New Testament the gospel writers note that their news fulfills a prophecy, suggesting that what they are offering as news is what they have read in Micah, or Jeremiah, or Isaiah. It may not be something that actually happened the way it is described or it may not even have happened at all. The prophets of the Old Testament wrote of the coming of a deliverer they refer to as a Messiah who would liberate Israel. And the writers of the gospels have slanted their accounts to fit the idea that Christ is that Messiah and to show that the prophets were right.

You have to notice also, Charlie, that the gospels, Matthew, Mark, and Luke, from which we learn of the life of Jesus, were selected from a number of possible texts. Other versions of the story not included in the Bible as we have it are known as the Gnostic gospels, and they sometimes give a version of events different from what is given in the New Testament.

Then, second, you must understand that many of the things we associate with Christmas are not to be found in the gospel reports at all because they have come down to the present day from pagan origins and have been blended into the story of the birth of Christ. The word pagan is used for a person who was neither Christian nor Jew. I'm using it to mean the people who lived before Christ, perhaps a long time before. It is not used in any belittling way, not a put-down, as it may be sometimes with us today. Nor is the word primitive derogatory; these men and women in their own ways were religious. And some of the rituals they practiced have been adopted by Christians and blended in to our own religious activities. But at various times other parts of the pagan religions have, as you will see, been absolutely unacceptable to some Christians.

The mixture of paganism and Christianity is partly the result of a deliberate policy. At the end of the sixth century (that's the 500's) Pope Gregory sent St. Augustine to England to give a boost to the beginnings of Christianity that were growing there. (Note, Charlie: there were two Augustines: the earlier, more famous one contributed to the shaping of Christian beliefs; this is the other one, the missionary.) The pope told him not to destroy the pagan temples and rituals but to graft the Christian beliefs on to them. In one weird ritual, for example, Christian converts were to eat a huge number of oxen; they had previously done so in honor of a pagan god; Augustine told them they were to go ahead and do the same thing but now for the glory of the Christian God. It was a kind of Christian infiltration. And so among our Christmas activities, though we don't go for all that beef any more, there are some which have no real relation at all to the birth of Christ but have been added on from ancient traditional rituals, religious but pagan, which go back many centuries before the birth of Christ. When the Puritans came to control life in the seventeenth century here and in England, the pagan parts of the Christmas celebrations became a reason for prohibiting Christmas altogether.

THE PLACE AND DATE OF THE NATIVITY

Luke reports that at the time of Christ's birth the Roman government ordered all people in the province of Judea to go to their own cities to be taxed. And thus, he writes, Joseph, accompanied of course by Mary his wife, went to Bethlehem. Mary was pregnant and near term, and her child was born in Bethlehem. You have known this all your life. But in fact the decree of the Roman government which was supposed to have caused the holy parents to take this journey was not actually sent out at the time of Christ's birth. And it is thought that the government decree was brought into the story only in order to explain why the parents were in Bethlehem for the nativity. And why did the story need them to be in Bethlehem? Because the writer of the gospel got this detail not from actual facts known to him but from a prophecy delivered some seven hundred years earlier by Micah, one of the prophets of the Old Testament, who had declared that Bethlehem was the place from which the Messiah would come. The Messiah was expected by the prophets to come to deliver the Jews and become their ruler. In his own day Christ was identified with this ruler, an identification he accepted, though profoundly changing the expected role. It is not known for sure where the Christ child was born. The gospel writers were not there; they did not know; they trusted the prophets. They probably got it wrong.

The next question is, what day and month in the year did he actually begin his life? Was it December and the 25th? The gospels do not say, and for some hundreds of years after the event the Fathers of the Church, those men in the early days of Christianity who dictated what Christians were to believe, argued and discussed the question of the time. What you have to understand, Charlie, is that for many primitive communities in the old world the end of the year was a very special time. Back then in the dawn of time, men and women realized that since vegetation was their source of food the cold which shriveled and killed it each winter was a threat to their own livelihood. And so they pictured the changing seasons, the mysterious cycle of nature, as the cycle of the life and death of gods: in the winter the gods died; in the spring they rose again from the dead. (One possible source for the word Yule is a word meaning wheel or cycle.)

One of these nature gods who died and was resurrected was a Babylonian god Tammuz. He was only one among others, but I mention him because his name comes into a beautiful legend I want to tell you about later. He died in winter; and in spring, when plants began to revive, he came to life again. The name Tammuz means the resurrected child. He was the son of the mother goddess of earth, and he was also her lover. (This sort of thing doesn't happen much in real life, and it will seem strange to you, Charlie. But with the old gods the arrangement was convenient and not too unusual.) Each year in the spring the mother of Tammuz went down into the underworld to bring him back from the dead.

In Greek myth there was a god closely related to Tammuz: Adonis. He was killed by a boar. But the Greeks believed that because he was loved by Aphrodite, the goddess of love, he was allowed to spend six months of the year in the upper world and six underground. So in this way, like Tammuz, he is related to the death of nature in winter and its revival in spring. As pagan people in Babylon and in Jerusalem celebrated the life and death of Tammuz, so in the Greek world people celebrated the life and death of Adonis. But the old prophets of Israel, whose god was Jehovah, the god of the Old Testament, the true God, looked on such gods as Tammuz with horror. And in a vision which his god showed him, the prophet Ezekiel sees some women at the gate of Jerusalem chanting laments for the death of Tammuz. And in Ezekiel's eyes the sight is disgusting, a pagan abomination.

So if we go back a long long way into prehistory, the dark backward and abysm of time, we find Tammuz and Adonis and other figures like them in the rituals that marked the beginning of the winter season in the last days of December. In the old days, these rituals were very widespread. Again and again, ancient peoples celebrated the season by acting out the death of a god in rituals that made sure that the god would revive in the following spring. Celebrations took many different forms: sometimes a model of the god was buried or thrown into the water or burned; but sometimes, the celebration took the form of the killing of some real person who represented the god—often a king or a priest. There are many versions of this kind of ritual in the primitive world; some people believe that their similarity to the Christian story, the murder of Christ and his resurrection later, give, in a way, some kind of endorsement, some support to the story that the Christians believed: the story somehow seems right, because it fits widespread, age-old human beliefs and the patterns of thought that have been stored in the human mind since ancient time. Indeed, it is claimed that Christianity spread rapidly in the Mediterranean countries because the killing of a god was not a strange thing to those peoples.

Later, in historical time in the world of ancient Rome there is a parallel to the priestly victim in the figure of the mock king, who presided over the celebration of the great annual Roman orgy, the Saturnalia, which was also held in December. Originally, the mock king was chosen by lot. He was made to represent the god Saturn, dressed up in royal robes, and permitted all kinds of things that were usually forbidden. Then at the end of his time he had to cut his throat on an altar. In later years, as the Saturnalia developed, the fate of the king of the celebrations was not quite so awful.

The orgy was seven days of fun. Businesses closed down, so did the schools (you would have liked that); executions were postponed (there was something for everybody); and gifts, often of dolls, were given and received. There was eating, drinking, and all kinds of wild behavior. And the business of the king of these occasions was to give commands to increase the fun. In later days he was not killed when it was all over. One interesting thing about the celebration was that during the time it was on, those Christians who were slaves were freed. Sometimes they changed places with their masters, even exchanging clothes; and their masters served them meals and got instructions about running the household. And it is this odd business, the freedom of the slaves, that has made some scholars think that December 25th was chosen for Christ's birthday, because it was a day when the Christian slaves could be free to celebrate. Perhaps that is how it was.

Another, more likely source for that December date is that it is the birthday also of Mithra, who is closely associated with and sometimes referred to as the god of the sun. In the third century (the 200's, remember?) the Roman Emperor Aurelian decided that the official god of the Romans was to be the Sun God. And that god's birthday was December 25th.

According to legend, the first living creature on earth was a white bull. The sun sent a raven to command Mithra to kill it. Accordingly Mithra, though reluctant, made a sacrifice of the bull. And then its dead white body became the moon, and from its tail sprang plants and animals. Then, too, day and night were separated; the moon's cycle and the seasons were created. Mithra went up to heaven in the chariot of the sun god, where his followers, those who had been baptized and had led lives of purity using bread, water, and wine that had been made holy by priests, were allowed to live forever. ("Grandpa," I hear you mutter to yourself, "aren't we getting a bit far away from Christmas?" Well, maybe so.) But notice that in his day, Mithra was worshipped by the whole world; he is worth knowing something about. And remember, as I told you, much of what we think of as being Christian goings on and Christian rituals at Christmas came originally from pagan practices.

The similarities between Mithraism and Christianity are simply extraordinary. In the Middle East those taking part in the ritual of the birthday of the sun, December 25th, at the time when the days started to get longer, would come out of a cave at midnight shouting, "The Virgin has brought forth." And as you may know, St. Matthew's gospel tells us that Christ was born of a virgin, a detail Matthew got from a prophecy in Isaiah. (Notice, Charlie, that the Hebrew word that appears translated in the gospel as "virgin" means a young, eligible woman. It may or may not have the meaning we generally attach to it.) So close and so extensive are the similarities between Mithraism and Christianity that Tertullian, the church father between the second and third centuries, explained the Mithraic rituals as a deliberate parody of Christianity inspired by the devil.

The cult of Mithra, which began in India fourteen hundred years before the birth of Christ was popular in Rome up until the fourth century of the Christian era, especially in the army; and it spread across the empire. The sun's birthday was one of the most popular festivals, and Christians had regularly taken part in it. So the Christian Fathers, after a lot of going to and fro about the matter, decided in the end that the nativity of Christ should be celebrated on that same day. St. Augustine persuaded Christians to continue to celebrate the day, not for the sake of the birthday of the sun but for that of the Christian god. By the fourth century, December 25th, the birthday of the sun, had been accepted by almost the whole Christian church as the birthday of Christ.

But it is not, of course, altogether likely that it is the actual date of the nativity. In the original story in Luke's gospel, ". . . there were in the same country shepherds abiding in the field keeping watch over their flock by night." And you will have heard various carols about how these men were out in the cold watching their sheep when the angel appeared and said "the First Noel" ("Noel" is an expression of joy. The word is usually related, as here, to a birth), and announced that they had good news. The "cold winter's night," which appears in the carol "The First Noel," is something added: St. Luke never said it was cold nor that it was winter.

What were they doing outside on that night, whether it was cold or not? Did they go out every night of the year to protect their sheep against wolves? Possibly. But one theory is that they were out there because the sheep were giving birth to their lambs. And if that is the case, it probably wasn't in December but later, in the early spring, that the angel appeared and then the unbelievably glorious pageantry of the heavenly host. The gospels are no clearer about the actual date than they are convincing as to the reason Joseph and Mary traveled to Bethlehem at this important moment of history.

THE THREE WISE MEN

While you were nosing around among the parcels under the tree when you were a kid, Charlie, looking to see if any of them might be the shape in which computer games were usually boxed, you would have noticed among the Christmas cards certain of them with pictures of three men, sometimes with crowns, riding camels. There was one such card from your aunt. One of the men was perhaps black. And you would have seen them also in the church, in the crèche, the nativity scene. These are the Three Wise Men, the Magi, sometimes called the Three Kings. St. Matthew, who is the only gospel writer to mention them, says they "came from the east to Jerusalem" seeking the King of the Jews: "We have seen his star in the east," they said. They meant perhaps, "In the east we have seen his star." If they came from the east, as they did, the "star in the east" would have led them not to Jerusalem where they were headed, but way off track—farther east, somewhere like India. Or perhaps what they meant by "in the east" is that they saw the star at its rising. For stars, as you know, rise in the east.

Herod, king of Israel from 31 to 4 BCE and a murderous thug, didn't like to hear of the birth of a rival, another King of the Jews; and he sent for his advisers. He wanted to know where this child was, in order he said that he too might worship him. He lied, of course, intending to kill the child. The advisers told him that the birth would be in Bethlehem, that town having been named by the prophet Micah.

So Herod sent the Three Wise Men to Bethlehem to check up on the baby. And, as we read, "the star which they had seen in the east went before them till it came and stood over where the young child was. When they saw the star, they rejoiced." That the star moved to the south (Bethlehem is south of Jerusalem) and then remained stationary over Bethlehem is unlikely: stars don't do that. It might have been the conjunction of two circling planets or a comet that appeared to have stopped moving, or perhaps a nova, the sudden brightening of a star that had not before been observed. Or the star might have appeared to have stopped when the men stopped; but if so, the star was following the men and not the men the star. Anyway, the movement of the star is perhaps an imaginary addition to the bare facts, the kind of improvement that historians in all ages have made. But the gospel writer's interest in the star is important.

The Three Wise Men are thought to have been from Persia, the country now known as Iran. They were priests of a religion called Zoroastrianism. It was some two hundred years after Christ's birth that the Church Father Tertullian declared they were kings, or near-kings. If they were Zoroastrian priests they belonged anyway to the highest level of Persian society. They were followers of the prophet Zoroaster who lived at some time in the five hundred years between 1000 and 500 BCE. It was a period of some hundreds of years that produced, as well as Zoroaster, other great spiritual leaders: Gautama Buddha, Confucius, and Socrates. (It has been said that in that epoch men and women became more religious than earlier. I'm not sure about that. Who can speak for the whole human race? Besides I hear you say again, "Come on, Grandpa; let's get back to Christmas.")

Well then, the students of the Zoroastrian religion were taught in those days that some time in the future a prophet would be born, the son of a virgin, and when he was born there would be a star so bright that it would be visible not only at night but in the noonday sun. Thus the priests were to follow this star until they came upon the new-born baby, and they were to offer him costly gifts and to bow down before him.

Once again Zoroastrianism was curiously similar to Christianity in many ways, and in fact certain Christian beliefs came originally from the Zoroastrians via the Jews. The Jews who had been held captive in Babylon were freed by a Persian king, Cyrus, who conquered Babylon in 539

BCE. Cyrus was a Zoroastrian, and the Jews took from him certain ideas that became incorporated in their religion: the ideas of judgment, of immortality, of the resurrection of the body, and the ideas of heaven and hell.

The Zoroastrian religion was dualistic: it held that there was a continual war going on between the light and the dark, between Mazda, the spirit of goodness represented by fire, and Ahriman, the spirit of darkness. And this war was fought out in a man's soul. The Zoroastrian belief that is of interest to the Christian story we are following was that each good man has in heaven a guardian spirit, a kind of higher soul which shared his life, guided him, and when he died was united with the soul that he had carried with him throughout his life on earth. At the birth of a great man the guardian spirit appeared as a star in the sky; if he was a very great man, it was a very bright star. So the Zoroastrian priests, the Wise Men, followed the star of the Christ child, and worshipped him. They were the first non-Jews to do so.

The gifts of the wise men were gold, frankincense, and myrrh. Frankincense and myrrh are both gums produced by certain eastern trees and shrubs. The gold was given by Melchior, because the child was royal; the frankincense by Balthazar, because the child was divine; the myrrh, by Gasper, because he was human. According to which story you read, either Balthazar or Gasper was black.

In their old age, the Three Wise Men were baptized Christians by St. Thomas. In 326, when she was very old, Helena, the Mother of Constantine, the first Roman Emperor to become a Christian, journeyed to Palestine, where she is said to have discovered the cross on which Christ was crucified, the nails too, and the tomb in which he was buried. It is said also that she brought the remains of the Three Wise Men—-the skulls in particular are mentioned—to Constantinople, the city now known as Istanbul. From there they were taken to Milan by Eustathius, the bishop of Antioch. Then in 1162, after he had captured Milan, Frederick, the Holy Roman Emperor, sent them to Cologne cathedral. As we shall see, an old carol refers to this part of the story.

When the Arabs overran Persia, Zoroastrian refugees settled in India around Bombay, where they are known as Parsees.

The Wise Men did not give Herod the information he wanted. They had been warned in a dream of his intentions and went home a different way in order to avoid him. Then, according to the gospel story though it is not supported by later history, because he could not tell which recently born child was to become king of the Jews, Herod gave orders for a wholesale massacre of infants. The action is celebrated today in the Feast of the Innocents, December 27. A legend has added that Herod's own child was killed in the slaughter. But at least one son, Herod Antipas, was preserved and lived on to mock Jesus just before the crucifixion.

2

Accessories to the Christmas Story

THE HOLLY, THE IVY, AND THE MISTLETOE

AMONG THE Christmas rituals which originally had no relation to the birth of Christ is the practice of bringing holly into the house. This comes from a part of the Roman Saturnalia, which in turn came from the prehistoric tradition of bringing green boughs into the house at the winter solstice, the tradition that made sure that the living principle in vegetation should be preserved from the cold and kept alive to be reawakened the following spring. The old carol, "O Tannenbaum," which goes back to times before the birth of Christ, has had Christian words added to it, but it harks back to this same idea: "O fir tree, you bear a green leaf both in winter and in summer." Among Christmas carols holly is associated with ivy, holly often symbolizing the male and ivy the female principle.

In one old tradition it was unlucky to bring in the holly before Christmas Eve. And it was thought also that if the holly had smooth bark it meant that the wife was the boss in the house; if rough, the husband. You may think, Charlie, that the holly with a rough bark is a pretty rare commodity; but you're not supposed to make jokes like this today.

In the past, however, many years ago, the question whether husband or wife was the boss was often discussed and joked about. And the story is told that once, some hundreds of years ago, when a certain knight was giving a dinner party at Christmas, he commanded that no man should get anything to drink until one of them who was the boss over his wife had sung a carol. For a long time no one moved. But at last one man half heartedly brought out the feeble sound of a song. Next the knight told the women that none of them might drink until one who was boss of her husband had given a song. At once there was a great cacophony of sound, as they all began to sing together.

Among the Christmas rituals, especially among the carols, we find that thoughts of the death of Christ are sometimes mixed in with the thoughts of his birth. Myrrh, like the gift brought by one of the Three Wise Men, was used in medicine, and also burned as incense; in addition it was used in the embalming of a dead body. So also the holly, brought into the house following the old old practice, thus comes to be associated with Christ's death: the red berries, his blood; the thorns, his crown.

Another plant containing the life principle that plays a part in our Christmas festivities is the mistletoe. It has no roots in the earth but grows in the top branches of the oak tree, and it flourishes there in winter remaining green when the oak has lost its leaves. Both oak and mistletoe were sacred to the Druids. These men were priests in England, Ireland, and France. They were not only a religious establishment; they were the people who ran the community in the days of the Celts before the Romans arrived in those places. They were something like a combination of the civil service and the law courts. They dealt with civic matters and they punished criminals. These priests believed that the mistletoe, since it had no roots in the earth, had been sent from heaven. They cut it with a golden scimitar, an old-fashioned curved blade now generally thought of as an old weapon of the Middle East; and when it had been cut, in order to prevent it from touching the earth, they caught it in a white cloth. It was used as a cure for epilepsy and ulcers, and it was fed to cows to make them fertile. It was given also to women who were unable to have children. Since it grew up in a tree and came from the sky as a gift from the gods, the Druids offered it back to them in sacrifices.

Although the Druids were often hostile to Christians, it is not really surprising that with such divine connections the mistletoe should be brought to adorn a Christian living room in the most important Christian season. So, Charlie, next time you are maneuvering a girl across the room to get her under the mistletoe, you could tell her that according to the old tradition a girl who was not kissed under the mistletoe would not get married in the coming year. But you might also remember the Druids, whose thoughts were a good deal more pious than yours.

The idea of the holiness of the mistletoe was supported in the minds of the Druids because it grew in the oak, for this tree was also sacred to them as it was to other primitive peoples. (The word Druid comes from a word which means oak-wise). Peasants in Europe would keep an oak log burning for a year and light the new log next year from the embers of the old in the belief that it preserved the luck of the house and made the crops grow. The Yule log, traditionally not of particle-board impregnated with chemicals to provide a colored flame, but of oak, bears elements of this old practice, though now it is lit during Christmas and not in midsummer as in the old days.

The bringing in of the Christmas tree, like the holly and other examples, derives again from the old practice of bringing in the greenery to preserve vegetable life. Among many races in prehistoric times the tree was a symbol for eternal life. In historical times it is thought that Martin Luther first introduced the practice of bringing the fir tree indoors. In England it began as a German thing, coming first into fashion in the 1840's when the Germans, Queen Victoria and Prince Albert, set up a little tree on a table in Windsor Castle, beginning a tradition which was later to bring a sixty to seventy foot spruce to London as a gift from Norway. But in America among the German community it had been part of the Christmas scene some two hundred years earlier. Since the important thing about the tree was its green-ness, its original meaning is lost when it is flocked in pink icing.

Another, recent, addition to the Christmas scene is the poinsettia, which came originally from Mexico. (And, Charlie, please don't omit to pronounce the second *i* in that word.) In the 1820s the first American minister to that country was Joel Poinsett. But as well as being a diplomat, he was an amateur botanist. And when he found this gaudy plant growing in the wild he took cuttings of it back to his place in South Carolina, where it began its career in this country as a greenhouse plant. A legend about a Mexican peasant child connects these flowers with Christmas. Lacking a present for the Christ child at Christmas, she gathered a handful of weeds and laid them at the crèche in the church. Suddenly, so the legend claims, because she acted in love, the bracts at the crown of the plant (because the red of the poinsettia is in the bracts not the flowers) blazed miraculously into a vivid color.

The color of the poinsettia, like the red robe of Father Christmas (originally the English model for Santa Claus), served the Christmas card industry which began to flourish in England in the mid-nineteenth century, encouraged by the institution of that wonderful system, the penny post, that carried and delivered mail for a penny, without regard to the distance involved. At the end of each term at my school, Charlie, we each drew and posted a picture in which our name was coded. It was some such ritual that led in the nineteenth century to the exchange of Christmas cards. Cards, as you will have observed, present nativity scenes, or they show rustic scenes in which birds and furry animals inhabit landscapes of rustic beauty—primitive dwellings, snow scenes, leaves outlined in frost, as you have seen. Notice though, the robin, of which the red breast was formed from the blood of Christ when the bird was trying to extract a thorn from the crown. But it is not the picture that really matters; the simple fact of the creation of a bond between men and women is the point.

FOOD AND DRINK

Well, Charlie, as of course you know only too well, among the important things at Christmas there is food and drink, lots of food and lots of drink. We know about that. But it's not like the good old days: we don't have a great silver bowl as our ancestors did, holding gallons, yes, really, gallons of ale, spices, eggs, roast apples, cream, and brandy. At one time, such a bowl would be part of the wassail tradition (the word comes from the Old Norwegian *ves heill*, be hearty), in which people carried the heady stuff to the orchard and poured it over the roots of the fruit trees believing that in that way a plentiful crop would appear in the spring. Good heavens, Charlie, in those days even the earthworms could get drunk! The foodstuffs they had in the old Christmas celebrations must have been fabulous: the boar's head, carried in with ceremony and a red apple in its mouth (and remember that the boar, which in legendary times had killed Adonis and of which later the killing was a part of a sacrificial rite, in historic times destroyed the crops, was a pest, and was killed and eaten out of hunger). And think of the ribs of beef, the strong ale, the flaming plum puddings and the mince pies—and in those days a mince pie was made of beef tongues, chicken, eggs, sugar, currants, lemon peel, orange peel, and spices. No talk about cholesterol in those days. We sing about wassail and figgy pudding, but we don't eat like they did then: we are so concerned with what's good for us we can hardly persuade ourselves that getting really stuffed with a stuffed turkey and all the fixings is a Christian exercise! Well, I suppose it isn't exactly that. But a full stomach, Charlie, may lead perhaps, don't you think, to a full heart? Good food and drink perform their own minor miracles. Do you remember the change that overcomes the characters in the film "Babette's Feast?" How with all that wonderful food the villagers forgot their petty enmities and stopped quarreling? Or again in "Chocolat," when with those splendid chocolate creations men and women were mellowed into warm, unusual friendships. But let it be said right out: in this century we are conscious that there is something shameful about gluttony: we eat too much; millions of others eat much too little.

One kind of thing that some people have on their Christmas dinner table that people didn't have in the old days is crackers. Not the little dry things you float in your soup but things made of crepe paper and cardboard cylinders. You may not have run into these, Charlie. They make a small bang when you and your neighbor at the dinner table pull at them in a tug-o-war. As they are torn in half, the cracker spills out a little toy, perhaps, a whistle, a motto, a joke, and a paper hat. These fun things were first made in the middle of the nineteenth century, when an adventurous young baker in London was given a sugared almond wrapped in tissue paper. This gave him the idea, and he improved upon the model by putting a little slip of paper with a motto in the wrapper with the candy. Then, it is said, hearing the sounds of the wood in his fire place, he got the idea of making the little parcel crackle as it was opened, a development which involved, of course, an increase in the size of the thing. Next, in place of the original mottoes came jokes. And then came the hats and the little toys, which were sometimes quite elaborate. The crackers are now known all over the world. From the beginning of the last century kings and queens of England have had them, specially designed, in the royal households at Christmas. And in this country they have brought some frivolity to the Christmas tables of presidents, senators, mayors, and sundry other V.I.P's. In this small feature of the Christmas celebration, I think it is the paper hats, Charlie, that play the most important part. The jokes have always seemed a bit unfunny, but whatever the hat is supposed to look like—a crown, a policeman's hat, a fez (you know, those little chimney pots they used to wear in Turkey), or nothing in particular— in the spirit of the festive season you have to put it on. Scrooge's nephew in Charles Dickens's *A Christmas Carol* found in the spirit of Christmas the power to bring people in society together. And are not these silly hats great equalizers? Everyone, children and grownups, school kids and school teachers, rich uncles and poor aunts, saints, sinners, company directors, stockbrokers, state senators, judges, bishops, professors, prudes, and prunes, in such headgear all come together without rank or station in life, as if, in Dickens's phrase, they were all merely "fellow passengers to the grave," all equal, all looking perfectly stupid.

THE PURITANS

In its earlier days Christmas in the west was celebrated with a zest like that of the revels of the Saturnalia itself—-eating, drinking, the wearing of animal disguises, and general fun and foolishness. At one time in England, noblemen were required by law to be at home in their stately mansions at Christmas so that they could show some hospitality to their tenants. It was thought by some in those days that the comforts and delights received by the workers at this season would remind them of the blessings they received from the God whose birthday they were celebrating, though as a beneficial effect of overeating this seems a pretty long shot.

But these happy days, when the celebration of Christmas was full hearted and a legal obligation, something you had to do, and meat and drink flowed in the

manor houses, came to a sad end in the seventeenth century in England when the dictator Oliver Cromwell came to
power and the Puritans dominated the country. Then they
came over here and likewise dominated New England. They
thought quite rightly that the festivities had pagan origins;
they thought too, again quite rightly, that the festivities were
part of the Roman Catholic tradition. Two strikes against
them: the Puritans hated both. For these reasons and also
no doubt because it was such a happy binge, Christmas offended them and they made its celebration a punishable
offense. In England in 1647 Parliament passed a law forbid-
ding the observance of Christmas, and one record describes
how on Christmas day in 1657 a church in which a service
was being conducted was surrounded by soldiers and the
congregation arrested. December 25th did not become a
legal holiday in the United States until the middle of the
nineteenth century. But then, even after it had been delivered from the cold thin hands of the Puritans, Christmas
still lacked something; it never regained the raw liveliness
of its origins and the earlier full-blooded joy in the fun.
And you will notice that among carols and the Christmas
festivities that came after the Puritan clamp-down there
is often a glance back to earlier celebrations, like, for example, the way Sir Walter Scott writes of Christmas in his
poem *Marmion*: "*England was merry England when / Old
Christmas brought his sports again.*" It's not "*England is,*" but
"*England was merry . . .*" Dickens, in the nineteenth century, is said to have brought back something of the fun of
the season. But even so, as we shall see, the pure Christmas
joy in Dickens is clouded with social concerns. Perhaps it
ought to be so; perhaps it always ought to have been.

SANTA CLAUS

And now old Santa, the jolly friend of all the kids, the old bewhiskered elf who comes sledding through the cold night watches and delivers toys to good children all over the world, giving, giving, giving, like a tax-and-spend liberal. He was your Christmas hero, Charlie; or he used to be, until that night when you overheard your parents whispering outside your bedroom door. He gets his name but not his belly from St. Nicholas, as you must have learned from the poem, "'Twas the night before Christmas," supposed to have been written by Clement Moore. When they colonized New York, the Dutch brought with them the tradition of gift giving at the feast of St.Nicholas. The saint's name in Dutch was San Nicolaas, which became shortened in this country to Santa Claus. By the name Santa Claus he is addressed each year by hundreds of thousands of kids whose letters are fielded by the post office. In England the character used to be Father Christmas, and their common ancestry goes a long way back to figures in the Roman Saturnalia. Their most recent ancestor is St. Nicholas.

Nicholas was a wealthy young man living in the fourth century CE in Patara, which used to be a sea port in the south of what is now Turkey. It has been the custom in many countries that the father of a girl who was to be married should give money, the so-called dowry, to her husband. The story is told of a poor man in Patara who was unable to provide his three daughters with dowries; he would thus be unable to get them married and would have therefore to send them to a convent to be nuns. Secretly, however, Nicholas gave them gold. One variety of the legend records that one of the daughters, having hung a stocking over the fire to dry, found it filled with a bag of gold that had dropped into it from the chimney. Three bags of gold became Nicholas's symbol. From this legend there developed the custom of secret gift-giving on the Eve of the feast day of St. Nicholas, December 6th, a practice that was later shifted to Christmas Eve. And thus it is that on Christmas Eve St. Nicholas, in a very different guise, comes calling.

The saint was a tall man and, in the pictures of him, skinny rather than fat. Clement Moore's person had a little puckish nose and was plump with a belly that trembled like jelly when he laughed. And the idea of a fat, full size Santa developed, recently reinforced by his appearance (holding a bottle) in an ad for coca cola.

Nicholas, the historical character, was moved from Patara to Myra, where he was appointed Bishop, and where legend tells of other miracles he performed. Myra was part of the Roman Empire, and its Christians suffered persecution during the reign of the Emperor Diocletian, who sought to unify a fragmenting empire. Under Diocletian in the year 303 CE (though his wife was a Christian) the last great persecution began. One story, though not easy to believe, tells of an occasion when 20,000 Christians were killed after Diocletian had ordered the temple where they were gathered to be set on fire. He had churches demolished, Christian books burned, and clergy imprisoned. The persecution was more severe in some parts of the empire than in others. Nicholas was in one of the bad places: he was imprisoned and tortured and only released after the end of Diocletian's reign.

In 312 Constantine became the emperor, and he ended the persecution of Christians. They came to be tolerated, and Constantine tried to bring religion, now Christianity, into a working relationship with the secular state. At the outset of a battle, so the story goes, he had seen a flaming cross in the sky, inscribed "In this sign conquer," and he had been converted. He had earlier been a sun worshipper; and in fact he maintained his homage to the sun god even after he had made the Roma Empire Christian. St. Nicholas is the patron saint of children, of scholars, and merchants. He is also the saint for sailors, and many of the churches named for him are built within sight of the sea. Myra, where he became bishop, was on the sea coast in his day. On his feast day St. Nicholas is celebrated particularly in Bari, in Italy, where in 1087 his remains were taken after they had been stolen from Myra. There the foundation of a basilica was laid in his honor.

In thinking about St. Nicholas and the Santa Claus he became we must remember how, in the legend, one of the poor peasant's daughters received her golden gift down the chimney. And thinking of gifts, remember Charlie, that the great gift of Christmas is, of course, the Christ child himself. And it is possible to think of the chimney down which Santa comes bringing the smaller gifts as an image of the birth canal through which human children come into the world. (Psychologists find that in their patients' dreams the birth canal is often symbolized by a chimney.) And in fact in earlier days in France, it was the Christ Child himself, not Santa, who supposedly used to come down the chimney bringing candy to stuff into the shoes (not the stockings) of the children. It is an interesting thought, is it not, that when you see a Christmas card of Santa wedging his fat body into a chimney you are looking at an imaginary scene of which the idea may ultimately have come from the natural process of birth in a supernatural situation: the incarnation.

A LEGEND FROM EARLY ROME

There is a beautiful and interesting story, in which Christianity is seen not as blending with paganism as happened so often, as we have seen, but as replacing it. The story is based on the idea that with the birth of Christ the pagan gods left their holy places and died. One such god was Apollo, whose practice in earlier days at his shrine, his altar, in Delphos in Greece, had been to prophecy the future. Another God that died at this crucial time in history was Pan. The story is told by the Roman historian Plutarch in an essay about the pagan gods abandoning their shrines.

Plutarch describes how friends had been discussing the question, Can the gods die? when a grammar teacher, Epitherses, told this story. He said he was once sailing north up the west coast of Greece, on the way to Italy. The ship carried many passengers. One evening after dinner, they passed near the Echinades Islands, and the ship drifted near the island of Paxi. Almost all the passengers were awake when they heard a loud voice from the island calling out of the fog, "Thamus." Many on board did not know that Thamus, an Egyptian, was the name of the pilot of the ship. The voice called twice, but Thamus made no reply. After the third time the voice called, he answered, and the voice then shouted, "When you come opposite to Palodes, announce that Great Pan is dead."

The passengers were amazed and discussed whether they should follow these instructions and announce the death of Pan or whether they should leave well alone and ignore them. Thamus decided that if there were a breeze he would sail right ahead saying nothing, but if when they got to that area there were no wind and the sea were smooth he would announce what he had heard. And that was how it was: when the ship came opposite Palodes, there were no winds or waves. So Thamus stood in the stern of the ship and, looking towards the land, repeated the words he had heard, "Great Pan is dead." Then, almost before he had finished, there was a loud wail of lamentation, coming from a crowd.

When the ship arrived in port, since there were a number of people aboard, the news of the incident spread through Italy. Eventually it found its way to Rome and to the emperor Tiberius. The emperor sent for Thamus, and he became so convinced of the truth of the story that he had the scholars at his court make a study of Pan. They decided that the Pan mentioned must have been none other than Pan, the god. This was the son of Hermes and Penelope, the Greek god of flocks and herds, who in most pictures has a human head but a goat's horns and feet. He was in the habit of chasing young women and also of frightening travelers, from which practice comes the word panic. The voice pronounced him dead at the time of the birth of Christ.

Later, some scholars have suggested that the voice Thamus, the pilot, heard was not calling his name and the message was not that Great Pan was dead (in Greek, Pan megas tethneke), but that what he heard was "Tammuz, Tammuz, Tammuz the all-powerful is dead," the ritual lament for Tammuz who, as we have seen, died each year. The sounds, Tammuz and Thamus are close enough to be confused at a distance, and Pan megas (great Pan) and pammegas (all-powerful) are clearly similar.

But just imagine the scene, Charlie, the ship slowly dipping through the almost windless sea, the great voice booming through the fog, "Great Pan is dead," and then the wailing from the shore. It's a wonderful legend. And if it didn't really happen? Like so many other legends in the Christian story our appreciation of it ought not to be ruined by historical facts or their absence.

Plutarch, from whose history the story comes, doesn't actually connect this incident with any part of the Christian story. Some writers, the French writer Rabelais for example, have claimed it relates not to the birth but to the death of Christ, Christ here being called the Great Pan in another instance of the mixing of Christian and pagan stories. And it was, in fact, Christ's death and not his birth that occurred during the time that Tiberius was emperor, from C.E. 14 to 37. But the story may have got to Rome some years after the incident had happened, and the episode is often thought to have taken place just at the time of the birth of Christ, when, with the arrival of Christ, the true God, the pagan ones left their shrines and died. It was understood this way by the Church Father Eusebius, Bishop of Caesarea, writing his history of the church in the early fourth century. And it is thus accepted also by the English poet John Milton who refers to the story in his magnificent hymn, "On the Morning of Christ's Nativity," in which he describes how on this unique morning of history, the oracles were dumb and Apollo was finished: *Apollo from his shrine / Can no more divine* (prophecy) / *With hollow shriek the steep of Delphos leaving . . .* And then: *The lonely mountains o'er / And the resounding shore, / A voice of weeping heard and loud lament . . .* where the poet is remembering the experience of Thamus, the Egyptian pilot, as he sailed past Palodes.

Well now, Charlie, you skipped that last bit, didn't you? You saw it was poetry (maybe I shouldn't have put it in italics) and so you thought it wouldn't interest you. Well it should. So now you just go back and read it: sound out the words and *listen* to it! It's good stuff!

It must be added that, according the St. Jerome, it was some three or four centuries after the nativity that the shrines of the pagan gods fell into disrepair and became covered with dust.

3

Christmas and the Arts

MESSIAH

Now I want to tell you something about *Messiah*, Charlie, the music. I expect that at Christmas time when you were a kid, one evening you would have been hauled off to hear *Messiah*, the oratorio by Frederic Handel. I can imagine: "But Dad, do I have to? I was going to watch TV. It's my best show." And between threats and bribes (an extra hour before the hypnotic tube, perhaps), you were brought to the concert hall, sulking. But I expect also that, without admitting it, there were parts of the music that you really enjoyed. Now you are older you must try it again.

Messiah (both Handel and Charles Jennens, who provided the words, the libretto, referred to it without the "the") is an oratorio, that is a mixture of opera and church music. In a way the combination is a bit like what we have seen in other Christmas rituals, the coming together of sacred Christian themes and the non-Christian. But it is different, of course, because the non-Christian part here is not a pagan theme, it is simply that within the oratorio there is music from secular, that is non-Christian, operas. For instance, even within the great Hallelujah chorus itself, there are passages of music taken just about unchanged from Handel's Italian chamber duets where the subject is not religious love but Italian *amore*, ordinary erotic love, the kind you know all about.

Handel was originally a German. He became English in 1726 when he was forty-one. He was a young genius, who began to compose early in his life. At the age of seventeen he was the organist of Halle Cathedral in Germany. He left Halle for Hamburg where he played the violin in the opera. And then he spent four years in Italy, studying Italian operas, of which he was to compose more than forty. After his Italian stay, he was appointed to the court of the Elector of Hanover. Hanover was a state in what is now Germany, and the Elector was its head. But while Handel had this job he used to take long leaves of absence in England, which annoyed the Elector, who was later to become the King of England, George 1st. It is said that Handel made his peace with the king by composing the *Water Music*, a series of pieces that were played at a royal party on the Thames, the river that flows through London. It pleased King George so much that he forgave Handel for his earlier neglect of duty.

Handel was a lively man, not one of your half-starved, thin bearded musicians. You've heard of these poor guys, Charlie: all through history there have been painters, writers, musicians who, before such characters were fed by a professorship in a college or a grant from a National Endowment for the Arts, struggled to please an indifferent public and scrape a pitiful livelihood. But Handel was not among these. Though he twice went bankrupt during his career, he became rich. He was tremendously productive, and he was certainly spirited. During his time in Hamburg, he and a friend,

Johann Mattheson, journeyed to Lubeck at the time when Dietrich Buxtehude, the famous organist, was about to retire. Handel wanted the job. But he discovered that the successor to Buxtehude was expected to marry his daughter, and he decided he was not an eligible candidate.

Back in Hamburg he had another narrow, more dangerous escape. He was playing the harpsichord in the opera *Cleopatra*, composed by Johann Mattheson. Mattheson was singing the part of Antony; and after Antony died, he expected to go into the orchestra to play the accompaniment of the remaining scenes. But Handel would not give up his place. The disagreement led to a quarrel, and the quarrel to a duel in which Mattheson made a deadly sword thrust at Handel. The thrust was stopped by a button on Handel's coat, which saved his life and saved for the world one of its most majestic pieces of music. Think of that, Charlie! If it hadn't been for that button, we would not have had the *Messiah*, and you, of course, instead of going out in the cold could have stayed home that particular evening, curled up on the couch the way you used, and watched tv.

As you can see Handel was a forceful man who knew what he wanted. And once when a prima donna , behaving in fact like a prima donna, wouldn't follow his instructions, he held her out the window, shook her and threatened to drop her until she gave in. Not the sort of guy to tangle with! But at the same time, he was a pious man who hoped to die on a Good Friday, so that he could rise with Christ on Easter Sunday.

His career in London began in 1710 with the creation of operas. But the Bishop of London and bishops elsewhere in England would not allow their boys' choirs to take part in theatrical activities during Lent. Thus Handel began to write oratorios, which unlike operas have no action and no scenery or costumes, only the singing. Handel composed *Messiah* in 1741. He himself spoke English with some difficulty and with an accent, and you will notice in the oratorio that he sometimes puts the stress on the wrong syllable or word. But the libretto is in English because Handel couldn't afford to import Italian singers. What's more, the Italian singers, unlike the English soloists, wanted to personally dominate the music. The operatic roles they had sung had called for their own personal flamboyance and self promotion in the music, he or she wanting to be the star of the performance, naturally enough, I suppose. With the more modest English soloists, on the other hand, it is the oratorio as a whole that calls for our attention, not the individual singing parts. They are, most of them, incredibly beautiful; but they are, each of them, merely a contribution to the total effect.

Handel didn't think of *Messiah* as an especially Christmas oratorio, and it was first performed at Easter in 1742 in Dublin, Ireland. It is we, not Handel, who have chosen to make it a part of Christmas. Its first complete performance in the United States was on Christmas Day 1818, though excerpts from it had been played earlier. Although it was neglected for a time, the work is now, two and a half centuries after it was first performed, still kept in the very front of the public awareness.

When it was first performed the Dublin audiences were enthusiastic. The response was so great that one newspaper urged ladies who were planning to attend the concert to wear their narrow skirts rather than their hooped ones and gentlemen to go without their swords so that an additional hundred people could be accommodated.

In London, in 1743, the oratorio was not at first well received. A hundred years later, in the Victorian period, it was played in the Crystal Palace to a crowd of eighty-seven thousand by an orchestra of five hundred instruments and four thousand voices. By then it had obviously made its huge place in the world of music (though the manner of its performance in the Crystal Palace might not have pleased the composer). In London in the very beginning it was attacked by Puritans who felt it was not proper for a religious performance to be given in the theater, the arena of wickedness. . And it was boycotted by the upper classes, in those days as tasteless in their manners as they were corrupt in their morals. They were prejudiced against the composer first because he was foreign; but in addition he had annoyed society years earlier, because, being too proud and independent to bow down before the wishes of fashionable society, he had neglected to employ one of its favorite singers. Now high society paid boys to go round town tearing down the posters that announced the performances. It is true that in Covent Garden at the first performance of the oratorio in London the old King George II was so moved in the Hallelujah chorus by the passage "For the Lord God omnipotent reigneth," that he clambered to his feet, thus obliging the audience to do the same and starting a custom which has survived. (Another version of the occasion has it that hearing "And he shall reign for ever and ever," the king got on his feet thinking the words referred to him.) The king, however, a German himself, was not popular either. And it was six years before the oratorio began to be accepted and indeed praised. Here as everywhere, prejudice and narrow religious principles prevented the performance of superb music.

Much of the opposition to the oratorio was overcome when it became known that Handel was giving his profits to charity. On a number of occasions he presented the oratorio in the Foundling Hospital, a place where unwanted children could be deposited. In 1749, although he had recently been through bankruptcy, he gave an organ to the chapel of the institution, which benefited marvelously from the audience receipts when the oratorio was played.

Its subject is not the birth of Christ; in fact it has as much to do with his death. Its subject is nothing less than the story of the salvation of mankind, a subject of which no one before Handel had attempted to make a musical composition. *Messiah* was sketched out in three weeks (Charles Jennens thought that Handel worked too fast, that he ought to have given some months to meditation before he started). The oratorio is called not *Jesus Christ,* but *Messiah*, the name used in the Old Testament for the leader, who, as I told you earlier, was to bring freedom to the Jews who were awaiting him. It tells the Christmas story, but this is only part of what it is all about. The story of the shepherds in the fields is related in three clear soprano pieces, but only a little time is given to the details of the birth in Bethlehem that are mentioned in the gospel and the carols. And in the same way, when he deals with the death of Christ, Handel doesn't bring in the details of the crucifixion as they are recorded in the gospels but uses the words of the Old Testament prophet, Isaiah. So that what the oratorio gives us is not the actual stories themselves of Christ's birth, suffering, and

death but what they mean. Handel's scope is the whole picture: the birth, the life, the death, *and* their total importance
to humanity. Thus the passages he uses come not mostly
from the gospel stories but from the prophecies and expres-
sions of faith in the Old Testament. On rare occasions the
oratorio includes characters and speeches; but it is not really *telling* a story, just presenting passages from the Bible.
There are passages from Revelations, the last book of the
New Testament, from the gospels, and from the writings of
St. Paul; but the sources of the libretto are mostly passages
from the Old Testament, the words of the prophets and the
Psalms. And these selected passages bring to the work its
tremendous power. You know what I mean? You just feel
the enormous importance of these words. Don't trouble
yourself too much, Charlie, with what they mean; the words
the librettist, Charles Jennens, has used in *Messiah* have
gathered to themselves their own mystique, a grandeur and
a majesty which don't really depend on what they mean, if
only because for so many centuries so many hundreds of
thousands of men and women have held them not merely
in high respect but in awe, or sometimes perhaps fear.

There is no one authentic score for *Messiah;* Handel
changed it each time it was played. One or two places I
particularly want you to notice. You will hear, for instance,
how often the music reinforces what the words are saying,
sometimes quite obviously. The choice of a soprano or a
bass voice is closely related to the statement; major and
minor keys are similarly related to the statements in the
words. In the part "All we like sheep have gone astray," in
the very word astray itself you hear the music going wild,
going astray. Notice also that the triumphant chorus, "Lift

up your heads, O ye gates," is in a major key and the music, reflecting the meaning of the words, rises consistently from "heads," up half a tone to "gates," a tone and a half to "up," and finally two tones up to "King," and then descends in stages. Sometimes you may also notice a great wave of relief rippling through the audience at this point in the oratorio. Then there is the great climax of the oratorio, the statement of the power and majesty of God in the Hallelujah chorus. The words come from three passages in the book of Revelations, the last book of the Bible. Notice how the word "Hallelujah" (it is a Hebrew word: *hallelu* means praise and *yah* is Jehovah: "praise the Lord") beats its way through the first part. It gives way to "For the Lord God," and then is combined with these words until they are replaced by "The Kingdom of this world is become the kingdom of our Lord, and of His Christ." Then in the end it returns again along with "For ever" as a repeated interruption. Notice also how "King of Kings" is repeated, coming back in increasingly higher phrases to a climax, like the rising tones in the chorus "Lift up your heads."

Later the oratorio dwells on the salvation of man, who because of Christ's death will not die. This section opens with the soprano aria, "I know that my Redeemer liveth." You need to know here, Charlie, what lies behind this passage: Handel would have assumed that you would know. The words come from the Book of Job in the Old Testament, at a climax in that story. Job is a good man and innocent; and God has thrown everything at him—a series of tremendous mounting pains and hardships. In the end, at last he cries out, "Why, do you persecute me?" Then at this point, at the very depths of his suffering, he makes his tremendous leap of faith; and these magnificent words ring out: "I know that my redeemer liveth." Never mind everything that has happened to him, all the totally undeserved agony of his body and mind and his loss of family, friends, and wealth; in spite of it all, he believes: he knows that God lives and that God will do justice to him.

This passage in the Book of Job is one of the great moments in the literature of the West. And all that sad sublime story of Job, with the climax of the outcry of his belief in God, you must try to bear in mind as you hear the music. But notice also that Handel doesn't overstate this extraordinary moment; after the statement of God's victory in the Hallelujah chorus, it comes not with loud basses and bassoons but in an aria in a clear, controlled soprano voice.

Now, Charlie, remember that it takes a bit of effort and energy not just to hear but to listen to *Messiah* (Imagine what it takes to conduct it!) But don't be too surprised if you find yourself letting the progress of the music get away from you now and again, until some lovely aria, like "He shall feed his flock," or a chorus like "Lift up your heads" or the Hallelujah chorus itself carries you down in the flood and brings you back to the music.

I've spent a lot of your time on *Messiah*, because I think it is one of those experiences in your life that live in and color the deep memory, like some passages of Shakespeare or Wordsworth, or, for that matter, the first time you saw the Grand Canyon or stepped into the cathedral in Chartres, or other experiences that words cannot contain.

It demands attention.

THE NUTCRACKER SUITE

Another event that we have made part of the Christmas season, a musical event but with music a world away from Handel's *Messiah,* is the *Nutcracker* ballet. It is in no way related to the biblical story of Christmas, but it is set on Christmas Eve and its opening act has the familiar features of the season—the tree, the gifts, and the important part played by children, who all the way through are a major feature. At Christmas it is played at hundreds of theaters in this country and hundreds in Europe. It was first performed, along with Tchaikovsky's one-act opera *Iolanthe*, at the Maryinsky Theater in St. Petersburg, at Christmas in 1892. There were eleven performances, and then it was not played again in Russia until 1919, after the composer had died. Then it was played in London in 1934 and came to this country in 1940, played by the San Francisco Ballet.

The music for the ballet was composed by Piotr Tchaikovsky, who was born in Russia in 1840 and died at the age of fifty-four, after a fairly short but very productive life. If he had known the troubles that the ballet was to give him he would probably not have agreed to compose it. In the end, of course, after he had warned the ballet's director that he could not meet the deadline that had been set, it was a great success.

As we shall see, something of the problem Tchaikovsky faced lay in the difficult material itself that he was given to work with. But his troubles came from sources beyond the composition itself. They were due in part to the periods of depression he suffered throughout his life; and these were caused, perhaps, by the loss of his mother when he was fourteen, by a bad marriage, or perhaps by the guilty secret of his sexual style in those days when homosexuality was criminal (he could have been sent to Siberia). Or again perhaps his depression had no one particular source but was no more (and no less) than the usual kind of price that, if you are a sensitive genius, life may make you pay.

He was trained in the School of Jurisprudence, and his association with that institution brought a grim sequel. He began his adult life at the age of nineteen as a government clerk in the Ministry of Justice. But when he was twenty-three he gave up his job in order to devote himself completely to music. It was a rash move, because it meant he was giving up his only means of making a living. But over the following quarter century of his musical career in the long procession of superb musical works, including the *Pathétique* symphony, which is perhaps one of the three most popular works ever composed, the bet paid off. In the end, looking back, nothing is safer than a bet that has been won. At the time, though, it was a risk.

During his life in music he experienced successes and happiness, disappointments and distress in the usual proportions for a creative artist. Sometimes audiences cheered; sometimes they hissed. Sometimes he was confident, other times afraid and shy—the first time he conducted an orchestra he was terrified that his head might fall off, and so all through the performance, with the hand that wasn't conducting, he held on to his head by his beard. In addition to imaginary perils, sleepless nights, and morbid haunting fears he seems to have suffered a great deal of ordinary physical illness.

His death was the subject of a number of improbable stories, and only quite recently a horror story has emerged that finds it was suicide, the result of an outrageous, terrible, and cruel bargain. Following much controversy over the circumstances, it is now discovered that a report of his sexual affair with a young nobleman was to be sent to the Tsar. To avoid dishonor falling upon the institution of which he had been a student, a group of fellow ex-students agreed to hold up the letter if Tchaikovsky would kill himself. Accordingly arsenic was procured, and accordingly he took it. In order to make his death seem other than suicide, in public he drank a glass of unboiled water, so that it would look as if he had contracted cholera which was taking its toll in the city at the time. When he died, sixty thousand people applied for tickets for the funeral. Tchaikovsky was fifty-three; Bach died at sixty-five; Stravinsky at eighty-nine; Sibelius at ninety-two. Consider, Charlie, the loss incurred by the world of music when for a servile genuflection toward the pale honor of that insignificant school the composer of the *Pathétique* was condemned to death.

When you hear the sweet dance music of the *Nutcracker*, Charlie, you don't think of all the composer's various devils. But that's often the way it is with the various kinds of artists—painters, writers and musicians—whose art seems to be fed by the pains of the creator.

While working on the music for the ballet, Tchaikovsky wrote to a friend that he was suffering from old age, his teeth and his hair were falling out, and he felt his musical ability had left him. He said also that he was suffering from nightmares, both day and night, in which characters from the *Nutcracker* story pursued him and horrified him, teasing him, telling him that he would be unable to deal with them. And these sorrows, imaginary and real, made his work on the ballet a burden.

But a part of his trouble with the ballet clearly lay in the story Tchaikovsky started with. Even as a children's story it is pretty thin stuff. Originally written by E. T. A. Hoffmann, *The Nutcracker and the Mouse King* has been called the story of a good kid who is rewarded with candy. The ballet begins in the living room of the Silberhaus family, where the parents and two children, Clara and Fritz, are decorating the tree. The atmosphere changes as there enters upon this festive scene the children's godfather, Drosselmeyer, an ugly man with a black eye patch, who brings toys, of which the most important one is a nutcracker in the form of a doll. You need to know, Charlie, that the nutcracker, the little apparatus with which you crack nuts, has a long history. Carved out of wood, it was and still is often contrived so that the nut is cracked in the mouth of a doll of some kind, very often a soldier. The nutcracker as a military figure would not be unduly strange to Tchaikovsky's first audiences. Furthermore, early on in Germany nutcrackers were talismans, emblems of good luck, charms. Thus it is that when holding the nutcracker Clara has the magical dream that constitutes a large part of the ballet. The popularity of Tchaikovsky's work resulted in an increase in the popularity of the nutcracker dolls in Europe and America. Also, it was from about the time of the *Nutcracker Suite* that Christmas came to be dominated by children: it is *their* celebration, we say. And so toys of all kinds have come to play an important part in the festival, and their manufacture and retailing have flourished.

In the ballet, Clara is attracted to the doll and when Fritz breaks it she takes care of it. Later, when the house is quiet, Clara comes downstairs and fantasy takes over the story. She witnesses a battle between a regiment of mice, led by the Mouse King, and an army composed of Fritz's toy soldiers and gingerbread men. When the soldiers seem about to be defeated, the Nutcracker enters the battle. Then, as he in turn is about to be overthrown, Clara throws her slipper at the Mouse King and the day is won for the good guys. The Nutcracker then turns into a prince and leads Clara into a winter forest and a snowstorm. This concludes Act I. Tchaikovsky's brother thought the scene disastrous.

In the second act the two arrive in Confituremburg, Candy Land, where they meet the queen of that country, the Sugar Plum Fairy. There follow then a number of dances, put on in honor of the visitors. The dances have not only various national characteristics but also associations with food: the Spanish Dance representing chocolate; the Arabian , coffee; the Chinese, tea; the Dance of the Mirlitons (toy flutes), representing marzipan; and the Flower Waltz.

The difficulties Tchaikovsky faced which made him wish he had never started on the work were due to the libretto, the version of the story that had been created out of Hoffmann's original, which he probably felt was not really suitable for treatment as a ballet. The first act, in the Silberhaus living room, has some action in the gifts brought by Drosselmeyer and the quarrel over the nutcracker. But in the second act, we are taken into a fantasy, and there is very little action. Critics at the time complained that the ballet lacked drama, that it had no subject and lacked human interest. However you look at it, it's a pretty trite story.

There are moments of small drama, but they are not sensational. However, as you probably know, Charlie, in ballet the drama need only be small: enough story to make a frame for the dance.

When the ballet was first performed, in St. Petersburg in 1892, Tchaikovsky himself complained that he found it a bit boring. In this performance, the role of the Sugar Plum Fairy, actually rather a small part, was played by a woman reported to have been heavy, large, unpretty, and ungraceful as a dancer. All the same, she was apparently well received; and it was reported that the production was totally magnificent. Some of the actors were dressed to look like items of fancy bakery; others were in costumes resembling candy—caramel, sugar plums, etc. Everybody, including Alexander III, Tsar of all the Russias, recognized what a superb spectacle had been created. Tchaikovsky himself felt it was "too magnificent."

Many of the parts were played by children, among them George Balanchine, in his Russian boyhood, whose New York City Ballet more than sixty years later was to produce the piece. Tchaikovsky also employed children's instruments—drums, rattles, cymbals, and so on, some of which were played by the children. For the dance of the Sugar Plum Fairy he had got a new instrument, the celesta, "something between a small piano and a Glockenspiel," made by Auguste Mustel, a harmonium builder. Tchaikovsky had discovered it in Paris when on his way to the United States for the celebrations of the opening of the Carnegie Hall. He asked his agent to order one for him and send it to St. Petersburg, taking take care that nobody, especially not

Rimsky-Korsakov, should find out about it and introduce it before he got to use it himself.

You will notice how throughout the first act of the ballet the music is fitted to the action; light music reflecting gaiety; somber music the darker moments. And you will notice how not only discords but sounds of warfare accompany the battle. In other parts of the ballet, there are more subtle reflections: after the jolly music of the Christmas scene in the Silberhaus living room, there is a change in the mood of the music as Drosselmeyer enters. And when Clara comes back into the room at night the music again reflects her mood. If you listen carefully you will hear these musical effects. One contemporary found in the opening of the Waltz of the Snowflakes a relation between the high pitched notes of the flute and piccolo and the pizzicato (plucking of the strings) on cello and violin—between these and the feeling you would have if you were out in a snowstorm, cold and shivering. Well, I suppose if you turn your imagination loose you will perhaps be able to experience the music in this way: people hear what they are listening for. Another listener, with perhaps an even greater exertion of imagination, heard in the Waltz of the Flowers the slow growth of the plants coming up from their deep roots and gradually developing into a great explosion of blossom. Well, so be it. What you will certainly experience is the beautiful coordination of the music and the movements of the dance.

A CHRISTMAS CAROL

Charles Dickens published this novel in 1843. I know you have seen the story on tv, Charlie, but 1843 was BTE, the

Before Television Era, if you can imagine such a time. In those days, though, they had public readings: you would go to the theater and an author would read and half act out his novel. 1853, ten years after the book had been printed, Dickens started doing public readings of his novels; and he began with *A Christmas Carol*. The readings of that story made the audiences cry, which is not surprising since during the writing of it Dickens himself had cried. He was to read the story in theaters over a hundred times. There were also stage plays made of it in those days. In the early part of the last century one version of it was played at Sandringham, the king's country house in England. Later in the century in this country, it was read aloud each year by Franklin Roosevelt. And ever since its appearance, the story has been dramatized, filmed, adapted, and in various forms presented hundreds of times.

Dickens' story is very much a Christmas thing: it is said, if you can believe it, that at one time some people actually thought that Dickens had invented Christmas. And I suppose now thousands of kids in America know the story of how Scrooge, a miserly old business man, is haunted by his old partner, Jacob Marley, and is then led by three spirits, the Ghosts of Christmas Past, Christmas Present, and Christmas Future, into various scenes, which bring him to change his life. Scrooge! What a name when you come to sound it out a few times! In all his novels Dickens used amusing names for his characters, many of which have an only half-hidden meaning. For Scrooge, he perhaps had in mind the word screw, suggesting stinginess and cruelty. Cratchit, the name of Scrooge's clerk, suggests of course scratch: Bob Cratchit scratches at the ledger with his pen, and he scratches a living out of the miserable salary Scrooge allows him.

Dickens doesn't hesitate to make lists so that you know without any doubt what he wants you to know, and he tells us on the second page of the novel that Scrooge was "a squeezing, wrenching, grasping, scraping, clutching, covetous old sinner." But even if Scrooge was all these things, the voice that calls him an *old* sinner is not entirely hostile: the "old" softens the charges; Dickens is not completely unfriendly to him. And later we find moments in Scrooge's career where he is not just a horrible old man, as for example when he is witty: he tells Marley's ghost that he believes the ghost is only the result of indigestion. It is, he says, just "an undigested bit of beef," etc., "There's more of gravy than of grave about you," he says. The jauntiness in the character Dickens has created is made especially clear when the part is played by Alistair Sim, in one of the most popular filmed versions of the story. The human touches suggest that Dickens could not entirely dislike Scrooge, perhaps because he himself, who was always careful with money and keenly watched his royalties, knew Ebenezer Scrooge only too well.

In the end, as everybody knows, after what we would call his counseling sessions, the bad old Scrooge became the sweet old sentimental papa-bear who wanted to love the whole world and to throw money at it. And don't you have the feeling, Charlie, that Scrooge's story is one you've always known: the conversion of the bad guy into a good guy, the story we have wanted to hear over and over again all our lives? Even the Grinch who stole Christmas, horrid hairy beast though he is, gets the girl in the end.

We noticed earlier that Christmas, which in the early days had been a revel, a feast for all the senses, never quite recovered from its repression in the Puritan years. After them it became a time when social conscience and social considerations made their claims on the occasion, and there is no better example of this new attitude than *A Christmas Carol*. Dickens was a man of intense social consciousness: he was horrified and angry whenever he read about the living and working conditions of the poor, and worse, the working conditions of the children of the poor. Some years before Dickens wrote the novel, Robert Owen, a compassionate factory owner, had determined that no child under ten should work for him. But in general, children at the age of six or seven or eight were sent to work for thirteen hours a day or more in the mines and factories. They died quite early, and they were easily replaced by other children of the poor. In London at this time thousands of children died before the age of ten. For some months, when his father was in a debtor's prison, Dickens himself at the age of twelve had worked in a shoe-polish factory. Compared with the situations of many other children, this experience wasn't all that awful, but it was a part of his boyhood of which later Dickens was too ashamed to speak. Even now, over a century and a half later, we shudder at the thought of children working for long hours in terrible conditions. Think, Charlie, of the cramped legs and arms and the aching backs of those little kids! Think of yourself in one of those hellish factories or crawling through a coal-mine for long hours of the day. Think of them and be thankful your life has worked out differently! Dickens was certainly thinking of these kids;

he called *A Christmas Carol* a sledge hammer blow in favor of working children.

He was also constantly aware of the plight of the "children of the streets." He writes to a friend, "I have seen in different towns in England, and do see in London whenever I walk alone into its byways at night, as I often do, such miseries and horrors among these little creatures—such an impossibility of their ever growing up to be good and happy . . ." In the third stave of *A Christmas Carol,* (chapters are called staves), the Ghost of the Christmas Present produces from under his robes two miserable little kids. And this is how they are described: "They were a boy and a girl. Yellow, meager, ragged, scowling, wolfish . . . Where graceful youth should have filled their features out, and touched them with its freshest tints, a stale and shriveled hand, like that of age, had pinched, and twisted them, and pulled them into shreds. . . . No change, no degradation, no perversion of humanity, in any grade, through all the mysteries of wonderful creation, has monsters half so horrible and dread."

Again, Dickens knows what he wants you to know; and he tells you, leaving nothing to chance. But, at the same time there is still room for the imagination; and this description of these two poor destitute, dangerous kids leaves us with a much more terrible and powerful idea than some of the screen representations, such as the 1984 rendering of the story, the film in which George Scott is Scrooge, where of course the imagination is limited by the picture. Sometimes, Charlie, you get a richer experience by reading the book than by gazing numbly at the box! Remember that.

These children, the spirit explains to Scrooge, are Ignorance, the boy, and Want, the girl. Dickens thought of ignorance as the parent of crime; and he saw want, poverty, as the training ground for those who would eventually destroy society. He calls them "dread" children, and we know today a good deal better than Dickens did what terror and destruction can come as the ultimate product of hunger and subhuman existence. In 1853, when reading *A Christmas Carol* aloud, Dickens gave particular emphasis to the part of the story about the two children, and he regularly received a great burst of applause from a sympathetic audience.

The novel reflects also a strong sense of the evil of the city. As noted, Dickens habitually walked the London streets, and what he saw distressed him. In one part of the story, Scrooge is led by a spirit to a place he had never been before. Dickens says, "The ways were foul and narrow; the shops and houses wretched; the people half-naked, drunken, slipshod, ugly. Alleys and archways, like so many cesspools, disgorged their offenses of smell, and dirt, and life, upon the straggling streets, and the whole quarter reeked with crime, with filth, and misery." At this point, with its strong sense of the evil of poverty in the city, the story is nothing less than social criticism.

Also, of course the book is Christian. And one of the important lines spoken by the story-teller himself, reads, "It is good to be children sometimes, and never better than at Christmas, when its mighty Founder was a child himself." That line, spoken in connection with a game of Blind Man's Buff, offended some of its readers in Dickens' day. And some were also offended that a Christian story should be read aloud in a music hall, just as a hundred years earlier some people thought Handel's oratorio ought not to be sung in a theater. There are also the Christian sentiments of Tiny Tim in church, who thought that it would be good for people to see him, being a cripple, and think then of Christ who made lame beggars walk. "Spirit of Tiny Tim," the narrator remarks later, "Thy childish essence was from God." And of course there is Tiny Tim's memorable "God bless us every one," which as a kid, Charlie, that summer you broke your leg, cheeky as usual, you used to repeat as you clunked your way around the living room on your crutches. (We didn't stop you because the Tiny Tim business is all a bit too sentimental.) One writer made a version of *A Christmas Carol* in which Tiny Tim is healed at the end, an outcome which may have given Carlo Menotti an idea for *Amahl and the Night Visitors* in which the boy is healed after the visit by the Magi.

But social and Christian book as it is, Dickens knew what the ages knew, what we know, and what even Scrooge came to realize at the end after his conversion: that food is an essential part of the formula for new life, whether it be in a pagan ceremony or in a Christian one. Dickens was criticized for turning Christmas into a mere turkey dinner. But good food and drink in this book are a means toward a good end. At first Scrooge takes his melancholy dinner in his usual melancholy tavern and returns home to a bowl of gruel—a sort of thin oatmeal mush; but the Cratchit family, though they can barely afford it, enjoy a Christmas dinner with all the fixings and celebrate with enthusiasm the small luxuries which don't really fit their budget, relishing the best goose that ever was, the best pudding that ever was, and the best gin punch, in the sharing of which, gin or no gin, the children were included. Scrooge eats alone; the Cratchits eat together.

When the second spirit, the Ghost of the Christmas Present, arrives in Scrooge's room, there appears a mountain of eats: turkeys, geese, game, poultry, brawn and so on; then mince pies, plum-puddings, barrels of oysters, and more; apples, oranges, pears, and seething bowls of punch. It is a mouth-watering catalog, truly a hymn of praise of food and drink! Then a few paragraphs later, Scrooge sees the poulterer's shop, the shop which sold chickens, geese, turkeys, etc.; and its luscious contents command half a page. And then the grocer's inventory for another half page. And of course at the end of the book it is at the dinner with his nephew that Scrooge appears.

Washington Irving thought that Christmas "brought the peasant and the peer together." And Scrooge's nephew, also socially conscious, thought Christmas "a good time, a kind, forgiving, charitable, pleasant time, . . . when men and women seem by one consent to open their shut up hearts freely, and to think of people below them as if they really were fellow-passengers to the grave, and not another race of creatures bound on other journeys." So, thinking of Christmas as rubbing out the lines that separate us from each other, the lines between rich and poor, between masters and workers, we must remember how way way back in the Roman Saturnalia, with which Christmas, besides the date of Christmas Day, has its distant link, masters and slaves changed places. And even as Christmas seemed to these two people, Washington Irving and Scrooge's nephew, the one real the other fictitious, so the story itself, *A Christmas Carol*, has seemed to others to be doing the same thing, the book itself bringing people together, as one writer put it, "in friendship and love and fullness of heart."

4

Another Celebration

HANUKKAH

O N A day in late November or in December (depend-
ing on how Kislev the third month of the Jewish year
relates to the Christian calendar) begins another celebration. Hanukkah, the Jewish Feast of Lights, lasts for eight
days. On the first day the celebrants light one candle; on the
second day, two; and so on. Each night Psalms 113 through
118, the Hallel (the word means praise), must be recited.
The occasion is a celebration of the rededication of the
temple in Jerusalem (Hanukkah means dedication), which
followed a victory in 165 BCE that preserved Judea as a na-
tion and the Jewish religion and the Jewish way of life.

Many years before that victory, Alexander the Great
had conquered much of the land around the Eastern
Mediterranean. Thus for many years cities in that territory,
including those along the coast of what is now Israel, had
adopted the Greek culture; they had become Hellenized,
or, as you might say, Greekified. But for a long time Judea,
on the other hand, had kept itself apart from this way of
life; and the Jews had continued their traditional religious
practices. But in 198 BCE (remember you count the years

backwards) the Jewish state was taken over by Syria; and the Syrian King, Antiochus IV, made up his mind that Judea must come into line with the other states that had adopted Hellenism. So now in Judea, Hellenistic values—such as an emphasis on the individual rather than on the community, an interest in trade, in money, commerce, and wealth— began to take the place of the religious principles and the old virtues and values of the Jews. The Greek gods replaced Jehovah; and when the Syrian king demanded money, his soldiers stole the sacred vessels of the temple in Jerusalem. A statue of Zeus, chief god of the Greeks, was set up on the altar of the temple; and sacrifices were performed for him.

The story is told that an old Jewish priest called Mattathias, heard how Nicanor, one of the Syrian king's generals, had sacrificed a pig on the altar of the temple. Mattathias then made a dagger, concealed it in his clothes, went to Jerusalem, and killed him.

There was, of course, large resistance against the Syrian soldiers who enforced the new order on the Jews. Some of it failed: in one encounter the Syrian soldiers killed a thousand of a group of Jewish guerrillas who refused to fight on the Sabbath. Another group, however, which believed that self defense was permitted on the Sabbath, was successful. This force was led by Judah Maccabee, the son of Mattathias. The Syrians did not at first think his revolt was serious enough to worry about, and they sent only a small force against him, which the Maccabees beat back. Later, a bigger army appeared. But the Maccabees defeated this too, killing many and getting hold of the enemy's war materials which they badly needed. Then, at this point, Syria became involved in a campaign elsewhere to which it switched its military forces. This coincidence, which was considered a miracle by the Jews, gave the Maccabees the opportunity to take Jerusalem.

So in 165 BCE, after the statue of Zeus had polluted the altar for three years, it was removed and the temple was cleansed. The Macabees decided to rededicate the temple on the 25th of the Kislev, the ninth month of the Jewish calendar, since that day was the third anniversary of the day it had first been defiled. The celebration organized by Judah Maccabee was to last eight days. But when the Jews came to look for oil for the lamps they were to use in performing the rededication, they could find only one vessel that had on it the seal of the high priest—the seal, that is, that would indicate its purity; the other vessels had been polluted. So they had oil for only one night to light the lamps of the menorah, the branched candlestick, which was supposed to burn for eight nights. And yet the oil from that one purified vessel lasted through all eight nights of the celebration: another miracle.

Through the years it has been this part of the story, the miracle of the oil supply and not the military victory of Judah Maccabee and his army that has been the remembered feature of this seasonal celebration. Hanukkah is spoken of as the Feast of Lights. Perhaps this emphasis came about originally because later, when the Romans occupied Judea, they would not have liked to see the Jews celebrating a successful rebellion.

5

Two Kinds of Climax

SHOPPING

AND NOW, Charlie, we come to talk about that paradise, that blessed kingdom, where we fear no more the heat of the sun, where falls not any hail nor rain nor any snow, that place, like an open house in the evening where all men come. No, just kidding: not the Garden of Eden, nor any of those other perfect places, like Atlantis, lost under the ocean, nor the isles of the Hesperides where the golden apples grew, places toward which the human heart has forever yearned backward from this world of shock, uncertainty, and terror. No, Charlie, actually I'm just thinking of the shopping mall, that church of materialism, warm in winter, air-conditioned in summer, and glistening all the time with gaudy displays of perishable and imperishable goods.

The main life of Christmas and its meaning are, of course, quite removed from material things. Even the Grinch who stole Christmas and the Whos learned that. But that doesn't mean we have to quit shopping. No, as you know so very well, it is one great part of Christmas. And when you see the glitter of a shop window reflected in the eyes of a kid, or the kid in any adult for that matter, you realize that shopping is one of the rewarding burdens that make up the season. Someone in the family, your mother probably, your dad being busy with the football, has got to go out to the mall and elbow her way through the crowd to find presents for children, parents, aunts, uncles, grandparents, and for the kid who brings back the dry cleaning—don't forget him. I know you used to head for the stores yourself sometimes when you were a kid, to discover what there was there that you would absolutely need to possess when the after-Christmas sales came on and your dad had cashed you uncle's check for you. One Christmas I drove you to the mall, and perhaps you remember this scenario:

"I'm just about ready to give up, Charlie."

"No! Look, Grandpa! Over there: I think he's backing out."

"He's not backing out, Charlie; he's combing his hair."

"Look, he's got his back-up lights on."

And so like a falcon, hovering with wing tips trembling, we wait to stoop on our quarry.

As a part of Christmas the poinsettia has an American origin. So, probably, has the gaudy wrapping paper, which has the important function of making gifts look different and become different from ordinary bought articles. But the great American contribution to Christmas (and indeed to shopping in general) is the department store, and what a great and marvelous American thing it is. Everything under a single roof, so many bright shining objects, so much thinginess—you know what I mean? What a binge, a glorious wallow in the world of material things—some compensation, Charlie, for all the holy occasions of the season that you have been attending or have at least been threatened with.

Did you know there are stores in New York where as your fancy dictates (and your budget of course) you can buy a roll of Scotch tape or a helicopter? And how beautifully, blatantly, and absurdly displayed is all this wonderful variety, calculated to trap the impulse buyer even as the swamp plant engorges even the most cautious bug! But remember this: it's not all pure materialism: think of shopping for gifts for others as a ritual that nourishes and enriches human relationships, just like the family dinner at Scrooge's nephew's house.

Now, as I say, the mall is not an American invention. Basically it is a covered street, protected from cars and from hot or cold weather. In this country, and in England, and all over Europe after World War II cities developed malls. In many cities on the continent and in England the ground had already been cleared by the bombs of one air force or another. And from its earliest days it has been a popular feature with both shoppers and merchants. At first the swanky stores were not interested in the idea: they were standoffish because their customers were used to being able to drive or be driven right up to the door of the establishment in the Cadillac. It didn't seem quite the thing to have to *walk* when you're going to buy a diamond or a mink stole.

But as you well know, the mall is more than just department stores, shops, and the little boutiques which they carry on their backs. There are also booths for tattooing and for getting your ears pierced; people will paint your portrait or your nails; there are coffee carts, banks, and stands where they will engrave silver or pewter. There are machines that will dispense cash, sell you a phone card or a coke, or give you news about your weight, your blood pressure, or your future. And then there are the trees and benches, and old men staring into a fountain—there really has to be a fountain to be stared into—while other old men are playing chess. There are little kids romping in the monkey bars and big kids playing electronic games, and there are little old ladies in sneakers walking their daily quota with a determination inspired by the health channel on TV. The people who count such things report that most city people, at some time or another, go to the mall—something like 90%, and the reason they most often give is that it enables them to get away from cars—they mean other people's cars, of course. A lot of people like the trees and the places to sit. Some sit and think; some just sit. It's good, of course, that shops of all kinds are conveniently at hand. But the people who make statistics find that many people go to the mall not intending, not at first at any rate, to buy anything. They go because they want to see other people—a fair field full of folk, gathered from all the continents on earth—the people and the rest of it all.

For many the mall is what the church once was. People attend as people—different people— used to go to a church, either with a program of buying or of worship; or they just drop in to pass a little time in a congenial atmosphere. So take off the skateboard from your feet, Charlie: the place where you're treading is holy ground! Well, not exactly. But the architects who have been foremost in the construction of malls across this country have thought of them as being something more than commercial centers (though obviously the idea of selling goods has never been entirely absent from their minds); they think of them as places of community and consider them as not just a substitute for the church but as a kind of parallel. A number of simi-

larities between the two have been noted:[1] humans tend
to organize life around a ceremonial center, and malls like
churches are that kind of center. The geometrical lay-out is
sometimes that of a cross, like the nave and transept of a
church, sometimes that of a rose window.

Of course, it must be added that unlike the design of
a church, the lay-out of the mall may often be snake-like so
we will get lost and walk past many more dressed windows
than we had really intended. And within some of these store
windows are the most elaborate constructions.

The practice of creating window dressings goes back
to the nineteenth century when Macy's in New York began
to create the most marvelous tableaux, or sometimes even
moving scenes. Children and indeed grown-ups could stare,
as they still may, into a wonderland of toys, Santas, reindeer,
dolls, and candy against a magic backdrop of sparkling ice
and snow; a perfect world behind glass. And so today too,
getting lost in a mall is not without some charm.

The mall has it over the church in some ways: it is
open every day, while the church is frequently closed,
empty and dark, especially on weekdays. Like the church
the mall provides a "different space," and there is music or
at any rate muzac. There is also color, some sense of secu-
rity, and usually food, Fast Food, which can be a means if
not of grace certainly, but, as we have seen, of goodwill and
brotherhood. And at Christmas there is Santa in the mall.
You may be sure a lot of people go there, as a lot of others go
to church, and get some consolation. As you think of it, you
may be impressed by how like a church it is; but you may
think also how like a church it isn't. Anyway, it's certainly an
interesting possibility. Give it a thought.

1. Zepp, *New Religious Image,* 34–35.

CHURCH AND CAROLS

And now, Charlie, the climax: church on Christmas morning! There, as perhaps you will agree now that you are grown beyond the stage of presents and sugary eats, is the high point of the season: the glowing faces of the people, the greetings, the kids wearing the bright scarves and the woolly hats they had unwrapped that very morning, the decorations, the flowers, the holly, the organ blaring out the Christmas music, and the old familiar story in the old familiar words. And, of course, the carols.

The word carol comes from the French, meaning a ring, or perhaps from *carola*, the Italian for a ring dance, and in the beginning came from the circular dance of peasants in the old pagan days. Later the church, of course, opposed the singing, until, even later, it adopted the strategy we have already seen of injecting Christian themes into the pagan songs and rituals. Even now you can hear dance rhythms in some of the carols you sing in church. There are two sorts of carols: one, the kind that only celebrates festivity—the kind sung around the wassail bowl or when the boar's head was carried in and the kind that is closely related to the nativity story.

Carols of course, even the holy ones, were unpopular with the Puritans. And, like the celebration of Christmas itself, they were banned during the seventeenth century, both in England and in New England. At the end of that century, however, "While Shepherds Watched" was included in the English book of psalms and officially used in the English church. At the same time the individual chanting of psalms in unison gave way to singing by the choir, and church music was won for harmony.

In the old days, but still within living memory, carols used to be sung by the Waits. The word comes from an old German word meaning watchmen, and the Waits were originally the watchmen of the town and then later the town musicians. They would come round on Christmas Eve with their instruments—violins, flutes, clarinets, crumhorns (a horn with a bend in it, a bit like a sax), and oboes; and they would be given a few coins, not usually for themselves but for a charitable cause. They were a colorful group. You don't see them now except on Christmas cards.

Some of the carols you used to sing as a boy, in your little reedy voice, have interesting histories and legends attached to them. One of the most popular, perhaps *the* most popular, "While shepherds watched," I have already mentioned, wondering why they were out in the fields that cold night. Except for the cold, the carol keeps pretty close to the gospel story. We needn't bother about why the shepherds were "seated on the ground" or, in another carol, lying on it. These details were probably just brought in for the sake of rhymes. "While Shepherds Watched" appeared in England in 1700 and is said to have been written by Nahum Tate, a minor literary person, best known for his re-writing of Shakespeare's *King Lear,* giving it a happy ending.

It was a long time after this carol was officially admitted for use in the church that it was joined there by "Hark the Herald Angels sing." The words of this were written by Charles Wesley, who has embellished Luke's version by having the angels sing and not just speak. The carol is one of the more than five or six thousand hymns he wrote, whose brother John was father of the Methodist church. The music is Mendelssohn's. The words have been changed from

Charles Wesley's original. John Wesley, also a hymn writer, and Charles both objected when their work was changed; but they themselves sometimes changed the words of other hymn writers for their own purposes.

Can you remember, Charlie, when the name Wenceslas was longer than you thought a name should be, and you used to sing, "Good King Wences last looked out"? Well, actually in the tenth century there was a King Wenceslaus, of Bohemia, which is now a part of the Czech Republic, where he encouraged the spread of Christianity. He was a good king, known in his day as Wenzel, Wenzel the Holy. In the year 935 his brother, who disliked Wenzel's foreign policy, had him murdered. Later Wenzel was made a saint by the church, and his remains were taken to the cathedral of St. Vitus in Prague. In Wenceslas Square, also in Prague, there is a statue of him on horseback. In the carol the king is seen caring for the poor on December 26th the day when the Feast of Stephen is celebrated (Stephen, an early martyr, was killed by the Jews, because he accused them of killing Christ). The Feast, traditionally a day of giving to the poor, is still recognized in England as Boxing Day, when house-holders give the so-called Christmas box, a tip, to various servants and tradesmen.

The usual version of "I saw three ships come sailing in" asks "And what was in those ships all three?" and answers, "Our Savior Christ and his lady." But there are variations. And in one, a version collected from a boatman on a river in Northern England, the answer to the question refers to the relics of the Three Wise Men. After "I saw three ships," this carol goes on: "I axed (asked)" 'em (them) what they'd got on board . . . They said they'd got three crawns (skulls)

. . . I axed 'em where they was taken to . . . They said they was ganging to Coln (Cologne) upon Rhine . . . I axed 'em where they came frae (from) . . . They said they came frae Bethlehem . . ."[2]

"Away in a manger," is said, without much evidence, to have been written by Martin Luther. The cradle mentioned in the carol reminds us that during the singing of Christmas hymns in the early days, there would be a cradle standing on the altar which the priest would rock during the singing. The carol is supposedly for children, very small children at that; and the author, Luther or A. N. Other, has fallen into the mistake which we often run into in literature supposed to be for children: the belief that children really think the thoughts that the poem pretends they are thinking, when in fact it is the wishful thinking of the parents that is being accommodated. We don't really have such virtuous children or grandchildren as might be thinking, "Be near me Lord Jesus I ask thee to stay / Close by me for ever and love me I pray," or "Bless all the dear children in thy tender care / And take them to heaven to live with thee there." The lines are designed to please adults: the little kids don't have those feelings; they don't particularly want the Lord to be near their beds and they haven't really considered whether they wish to be taken to heaven to live with him. What they do know, as you yourself probably remember, Charlie, is that they want to be taken home to play with their new toys. So be it: the carols cannot be relied upon for accurate news of any kind. Another one, "Once in Royal David's City," provides a detail from Christ's childhood about which nothing for sure is known: ". . . through all his wondrous childhood / He

2. Keyte and Parrott, *Carols,* 517 n.

would honor and obey." The gospels of the New Testament say nothing about what Jesus was like as a child; one of the Gnostic Gospels, on the other hand, records that his behavior was far from "wondrous," and the principal of his school asked Joseph to take him away. The carol we sing ends with a commercial for the children, "Christian children all must be / Mild, obedient, good as he."

But even through the meager lines of such poems with their license and their misplaced sentimentality there glows something of the magic of the Christmas season. So too through all the other carols with their made up details, their doggerel rhymes; and so too through the little crèches—the wooden Christ child, the canvas cow, angels, kneeling shepherds, the Wise Men, the parent, and Joseph; and through the Christmas cards; and especially, of course, through the gospels themselves with their uncertain details, there shines that fabulous moment in history when men and women had to begin to grasp the extraordinary happening, the miracle of the god become human to live among them, the mystery of the Incarnation.

This word, Charlie, means the coming into flesh. The root of the word, carn, is in carnal, fleshly; in carnivore, flesh eater; in carnival, originally meaning goodbye to the flesh, the celebrations at the beginning of Lent when the joys of the body were to be denied; and in carnelian and carnation, flesh colored stone and flower. And the Incarnation is the coming into flesh of God.

So you see, dear boy, what a lot of curious and tangled sources, bits of history, legends, the scriptures, and pagan rites have brought to us the Christmas we know. And so from these same sources come eventually the gaudy lights on the trees, the neon reindeer on the roof, the shining stores, the salvation men with their little red buckets, the egg-nog, the rum-punch, the turkey and all the fixings (and the Alka-Seltzer), and the shopping and the traffic jams, and the living-room knee-deep in wrappings. And school is out and there are car sales and white sales and clothing knocked way way down by dizzying percentages. Why, even the US Treasury is in on the act, graciously declining to gather its quarterly taxes in December, so that happy people can buy things they don't need (and if the schedule helps business, so be it!).

When the wet nurses fed Queen Victoria's babies, they were obliged to stand up because they were in the presence of royalty—the babies! But think of the Christmas scene, Charlie, wrench your mind away from the tinsel and the toys and the mounds of food, and think of that part of the Trinity, the God, creator and Lord of the immeasurable spaces of the limitless universe, sun and moon, Lord of the planets and the stars and this round earth, the president of its massive storms, its upheavals, and its seasons, of its mountains, its seas, its forests, and all its peoples. Think, Charlie, of all the terrible majesty of the god come into human form in some obscure little town in the Middle East, incarnated into that little soft pink bundle in the arms of a country girl on the stable floor, sucking her milk. Perhaps it was something like that. Anyway, Charlie, think of it a bit, will you?

Well, if you have read this far, I hope you don't think your grandfather is a relentless old bore. But even if you do, perhaps some of the features of this wonderful season will have been made a little clearer to you, more significant, and maybe a little more wonderful..

Whatever! A merry Christmas!

Grandpa

Bibliography

Amiot, Francois. *History of the Mass*. New York: Hawthorn Books, 1959.

Baker, Margaret. *Discovering Christmas Customs and Folklore: A Guide to Seasonal Rites*. Princes Risborough, Buckinghamshire: Shire Publications, 1968.

Brown, David. *Tchaikovsky: The Final Years 1885-1893*. New York: Norton, 1991.

Burrows, Donald. *Handel: Messiah*. Cambridge: Cambridge University Press, 1991.

Coffin, Tristram P. *The Book of Christmas Folklore*. New York: Seabury Press, 1973.

Connelly, Mark. *Christmas: A Social History*. London: I. B. Tauris and Co., 1999.

Davis, John D. Editor. *The Westminster Study Edition of the Holy Bible*. Philadelphia: The Westminster Press, 1948.

Davis, Paul. *The Lives and Times of Ebenezer Scrooge*. New Haven: Yale University Press., 1990.

dePaola, Tomie. *The Legend of the Poinsettia*. New York: Putnam, 1994.

Eusebius of Caesarea. "La Mort du Grand Pan." In *La Préparation Evangélique*. Translated by Odile Zink. Livres IV–V, 1–17. Paris: Editions du Cerf, 1974.

Frazer, James. *The Golden Bough*. Abridged Edition. London: Macmillan, 1924.

Guida, Fred. *A Christmas Carol and its Adaptations*. Jefferson, North Carolina: McFarland, 2000.

Hodgson, Peter C. Editor. *The Life of Jesus Critically Examined*. Philadelphia: Fortress Press, 1972.

Hoffmann, E. T. A. *The Nutcracker and the Mouse King*. Translated by Louise Encking. Chicago: Albert Whitman and Co., 1930.

Holden, Anthony. *Tchaikovsky: A Biography*. New York: Random House, 1995.

Hole, Christina. *Christmas and Its Customs*. London: Richard Bell. No date.

Jones, Charles W. *Saint Nicholas of Myra, Bari, and Manhattan*. Chicago: University of Chicago Press, 1978.

Keyte, Hugh, and Andrew Parrott. Editors. *The New Oxford Book of Carols*. Oxford: Oxford University Press, 1993.

Kimpton, Peter. *Tom Smith's Christmas Crackers: An Illustrated History*. Stroud, UK: Tempus, 2004.

Larsen, Jens Peter. *Handel's Messiah: Origins, Composition, Sources*. Westport, Conn.: Greenwood Press, 1972.

Miller. Daniel. Editor. *Unwrapping Christmas*. Oxford: Clarendon Press, 1993.

Miller, Rex. *In Search of Santa Claus*. Turkish Press: Broadcasting and Tourist Department. No date.

Plutarch, "Obsolescence of Oracles." In *Moralia*. Volume 5. Translated by Frank Cole Babbitt. Cambridge: Harvard University Press, 1949.

Restad, Penne L. *Christmas in America: A History*. New York: Oxford University Press,1995.

Ross-Williamson, Hugh. *The Arrow and the Sword*. London: Faber and Faber, 1947.

Sandys, William. *Christmas Carols: Ancient and Modern*. London: Richard Beckley, 1833.

Sterba, Richard. "On Christmas." *Psychoanalytic Quarterly* 13 (1944) 79-83.

Waites, William B. *The Modern Christmas in America: A Cultural History of Gift Giving*. New York: New York University Press, 1993.

Walsh, William S. The Story of Santa Claus. Detroit: Gale Research Co., 1970.

Warrack, John. Tchaikovsky Ballet Music. Seattle: University of Washington Press, 1979.

Weinstock, Herbert. Tchaikovsky. New York: Knopf, 1944.

Wiley, Roland John. Tchaikovsky's Ballets. Oxford: The Clarendon Press, 1985.

Zepp, Ira G. The New Religious Image of Urban America. Niwot, Colorado: University Press of Colorado, 1997.

Printed in the USA
CPSIA information can be obtained
at www.ICGtesting.com
LVHW052350281124
797911LV00008B/338